Mastering
the
F·L·O·R·A·L D·E·S·I·G·N

A
step by step
guide

written by

THE
HORTICULTURAL
INSTITUTE
OF
SOUTHERN
CALIFORNIA

Roxanne De Palma
Floral Styling & Text

Lori Jacobson
Book Design & Text

Printed in Hong Kong

Published by
The Horticultural Institute of Southern California
P.O. Box 457
San Clemente, Ca. 92674

About
The Horticultural Institute
of Southern California

The Horticultural Institute of Southern California is a leader in the field of creative floral presentation. Robert and Roxanne De Palma, the founders of the institute are well regarded in the floral industry having been featured on national television and have been guest speakers at floral exhibitions around the world. Their primary goal has been to share their expertise in the realm of floral presentation so everyone can enjoy the beauty of fresh flowers in their home or office.

Robert and Roxanne De Palma, Founders

Contents

Introduction

At long last, and after much encouragement from our devoted customers, the Horticultural Institute of Southern California has produced MASTERING THE FLORAL DESIGN; a photographic display of seasonal and special occasion arrangements all created with the FLORAL DESIGN.

For your convenience we have designed each page to reflect a theme which is demonstrated with arrangements made of SILK, FRESH, and DRIED FLOWERS as well as FRESH FRUIT. The arrangements are easily recreated at home by following the step by step instructions included with each photograph.

Whether you are an avid gardener with experience in floral arranging or a novice who is starting to experiment with flowers, there is no doubt that working with the Floral Design will be a rewarding, fun experience for everyone that uses this product!

Floral Seven

Floral Design

What is the Floral Design?

The FLORAL DESIGN is a unique two-part, glass vase system for creating perfect, professional quality floral arrangements. The lower tier of eighteen vases is arranged in a ring with the height and angle of each vase perfectly positioned to create a beautiful bouquet every time. A clear glass disc accompanies each FLORAL DESIGN and creates a stable surface to add components such as the FLORAL SEVEN; our seven vase stacked unit, which when added to the FLORAL DESIGN creates a taller, more formal bouquet.

Care Instructions

To clean your FLORAL DESIGN & FLORAL SEVEN, simply place in the top rack of your dishwasher and wash as usual. If you prefer hand washing, use a quarter tablet of effervescent denture cleanser with water in each vase . To prevent the formation of residue, empty and wash the vases after each use. When handling a completed arrangement, always remove the FLORAL SEVEN from the platform to avoid tipping.

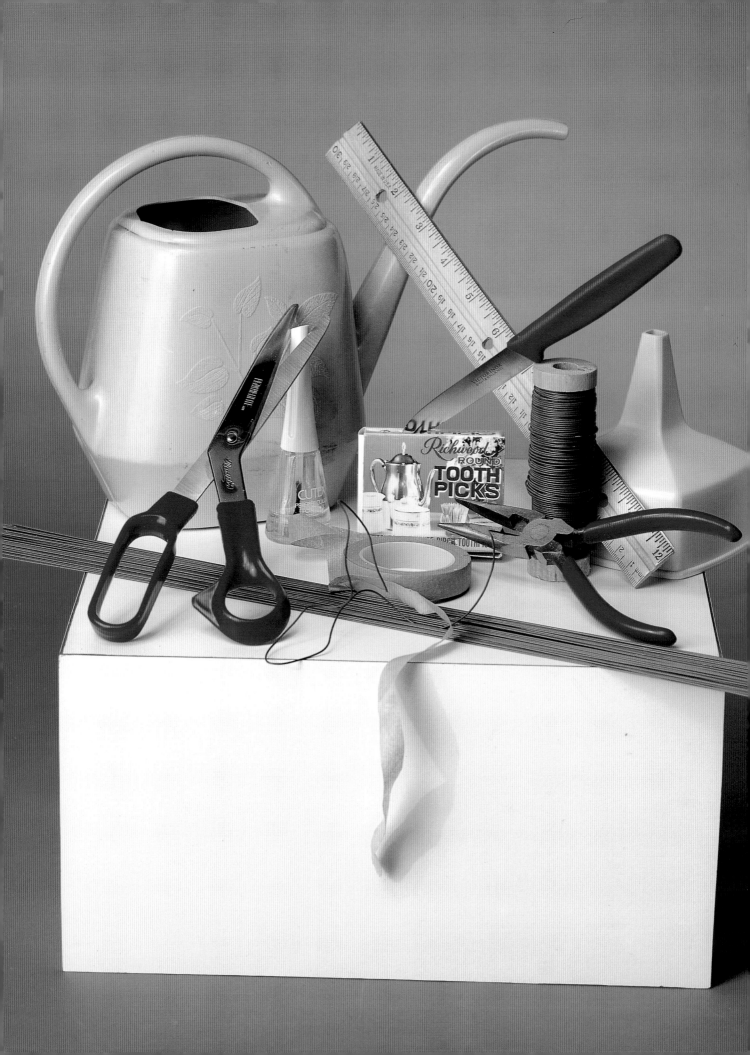

Tools & Tricks of the Trade

As we mention throughout this book, there is only one important rule to follow for creating perfect arrangements, CUT ALL THE STEMS THE SAME LENGTH! As you will notice from our list of suggested tools, they are common, household items with the exception of the floral tape and wire so you should have no problem getting started.

Listed below are tools and their use when working with the FLORAL DESIGN:

SCISSORS - Use for cutting all soft flower stems and any decorative accessory items such as ribbons or raffia.

RULER - Measure your flower stems and (once again) CUT ALL THE FLOWER STEMS THE SAME LENGTH!

WIRE CUTTERS - Use on all tough flower stems and naturally, on wire!

SMALL PARING KNIFE - A great tool for fruit and vegetable preparation as well as shaving the tough exterior off heavier stemmed flowers and removing thorns from roses.

TOOTHPICKS - Regular round toothpicks are perfect for securing fruits and vegetables used in the hors d'oeuvre arrangements.

THIN SPOUTED WATERING CAN - Use for easy filling of vases and daily freshening of vases without the inconvenience of removing the flowers from the vases.

FLORAL WIRE - Can be purchased in most variety or craft stores and is sold by the spool or in individual, pre-cut lengths. The most common use is to reinforce and strengthen thin, delicate or rubbery stems.

CLEAR NAIL POLISH - To prevent rusting of stems on silk flowers, dip the stem in clear nail polish to seal the stem. Once sealed the silk flower can be mixed with fresh flowers in water or embedded in soil.

FUNNEL - Use to fill the vases with dried anchoring material such as silica sand, cornmeal, grits, popcorn or any dried item that will hold flower stems.

The list above is very basic. As you become more familiar and creative with your FLORAL DESIGN you will probably discover your own favorite tools and accessories.

Elements and What to Work With

The FLORAL DESIGN has been created to accommodate the widest variety of floral materials available. In our photo illustrations you will see that we have demonstrated each topic with examples styled with fresh, silk and dried flowers as well as a topical food selection. Listed below are a few helpful hints about each category of floral material as well as some basic design information to help make your styling efforts rewarding.

SIZE - When selecting flowers, we suggest the bulk of your "feature" flowers be of medium size to balance the vase. Smaller blossoms and greenery should be treated as "fillers" and will help round out any open spaces as well as add color contrast to the arrangement.

Larger, showy flowers such as dahlia, peonies and roses, make a striking arrangement without the need of "fillers".

For delicate arrangements, selects smaller flowers and make mini bouquets for each vase. For example one cornflower, one sprig of baby's breath and a freesia.

COLOR - When selecting flowers for your arrangement, remember that color will have the greatest effect on the image you are creating.

To create feminine, romantic or pristine type arrangements use a **PASTEL** color palette, all the soft tints, tones and hues of a color. Pink, peach, cream, ivory, and beige are examples of pastel colors.

Drama or a more masculine theme can be achieved by using richer, more intense colors known as **JEWEL TONES**. Examples of these colors are ruby red, teal green, amethyst purple, and topaz gold.

High contrast and freshness can easily be created by offsetting **PRIMARY** colors against white. Primary colors are red, royal blue, and bright yellow.

LENGTH - The most important rule to remember when determining the length of your flower stem is: **THE LONGER THE STEM, THE LARGER THE BOUQUET**. Short stems will create a compact, more traditional looking bouquet, while the longer stems tend to leave more flexibility when creating a theme arrangement.

BALANCE - In traditional flower arranging, balance is very important but our **FLORAL DESIGN** vases have taken all the guesswork out of this area. Each vase has been permanently fused together at the proper angle to create perfectly balanced arrangements every time.

Preparation

FRESH FLOWERS - The most important consideration when working with fresh flowers is the selection of flowers, not just how beautiful they are but how fresh and healthy they are. Here are two key factors to look for:
1. Brightly colored, tight blossoms.
2. Strong, straight stems. (Flowers fade as they age, their petals loosen and droop and the stems bend, not the most desirable look for an arrangement!)

To prepare your flowers for use, just follow these guidelines and your arrangement will look fresh and beautiful for days.

1. Cut flower stems at a diagonal to remove sealed end and allow the flower to absorb fresh water. If you are preparing the flowers for later use, store the cut flowers in water at a cool temperature until ready to style.
2. Remove the lower leaves and any excess greenery on stems. Use a paring knife to remove thorns from roses.
3. Select the stem length you desire for your arrangement and cut all the flowers the same length.
4. Fill each glass vase with fresh water and style your bouquet!

SILK FLOWERS - The preparation of silk flowers is much less of an effort than fresh, but there are a few more considerations. The first is cost. The price range of silk flowers varies tremendously and depending on your taste, it might be wise to spend time researching the costs and selections.

Once you have made your selection, the rest is easy:
1. Cut all your flower stems the same length using wire cutters.
2. Dip the cut end of flower stem in clear nail polish to prevent rusting (Using silk flowers in vases filled with water creates a very realistic look .)
3. Arrange flowers in vases filled with a dry, easy to pour anchoring material like salt, silica sand, grits, cornmeal, even popcorn. You can be creative with the anchor ingredients, just make sure the density enough to hold the stems.

DRIED FLOWERS - The selection of dried flowers is almost as varied as fresh in today's market, in fact many home gardeners have enjoyed drying their own.

The most important thing to remember when styling with dried flowers is their fragile make up. Many flowers are treated with glycerin which gives them a little more flexibility, but generally speaking, dried flowers require delicate handling and become more brittle with age.

1. Cut the flower stems to the desired length.
2. For delicate stems, add a piece of floral wire and wrap with floral tape to reinforce the stem.
3. Arrange in vases filled with non-caking silica sand or salt mixed with rice to prevent caking. (The delicate dried stems are too fragile to force into resistant filler that cakes.)

FOODS - Last but not least we have the FOOD category, which requires the same common-sense preparation and handling as meal preparation. Select fresh, firm and colorful fruits and vegetables. Eye appeal is psychologically as important as flavor when it comes to working with food. Wash and dry the fruits and vegetables to remove any preservatives, soil, etc. Cut your fruits and vegetables to their desired lengths and immerse in cold water to maintain freshness until ready to style the arrangement. If using greens such as parsley in the vases, cut the stems the same length to create an even base for the food presentation. Place the greens in water as soon as possible to avoid wilting. Style the final arrangement as close to serving time as possible. The greens will remain fresh as long as there is adequate fresh water in the vases. The skewered fruits and vegetables will start to shrivel if left in a warm room for an extended period of time. To keep your fruits and vegetables from oxidizing, dip them in lemon juice immediately after cutting and they will remain fresh for hours.

The more time you take in preparing your flowers and foods before styling, the better your results will be. Neatly trimmed and groomed flowers and foods are the secret to professional looking arrangements.

TECHNIQUES
Fresh Flowers

We have compiled a variety of tips and techniques which we hope will be helpful in fine tuning your fresh floral arrangements so they can look as beautiful as designs done by a florist.

ANEMONES - Straightening Curved Stems
1. Wrap the flowers securely in a few sheets of dampened newspaper and secure with a rubberband.
2. Stand the bunch upright in a deep container of water and store overnight in a cool, dark place.

DAFFODILS - Buying and Conditioning
1. When buying daffodils, always choose bunches that are still in bud with the color just beginning to show at the tip. Daffodils that are in full bloom should not be bought because they will bloom out too fast and shorten the life span of the arrangement.
2. Daffodils exude latex which is harmful to other flowers. To condition the flowers, cut and slit the stems and let stand alone in water for 24 hours before using with other flowers in an arrangement.

EUPHORBIA - Sealing Euphorbia Stems
Euphorbia stems exude a thick, milky latex when cut. This sticky fluid can block the stem,preventing it from absorbing water, and can be harmful to other flowers in the display. To seal the stem, hold a lighted match to the stem or dip it in boiling water for a few seconds. This flower can cause rashes We advise handling the flower with rubber gloves if you have sensitive skin or allergic tendencies.

GOLDEN ROD - Buying and Conditioning
1. Buy golden rod when the flowers are still green and are just starting to open. If you buy the flower at this stage it will last up to ten days in your arrangement.
2. Cut the stems at a severe angle to expose as much stem as possible. This will allow the flower to take up enough water to stay fresh and healthy looking.

HYACINTH - Buying and Conditioning
1. Buy the hyacinth flowers when a few of the florets are freshly opened and all the unopened florets are showing their true color.
2. Cut the stems and stand them in tepid water for a few hours before arranging.

LILY - *Avoiding Lily Pollen Stains*

Falling pollen from the beautiful lily flower can cause serious stains on clothing. To avoid this problem, pinch the stamen between the thumb and forefinger while preparing the arrangement. If you are too late and have a problem with pollen on clothing, sprinkle talcum over the area and brush off with a clothes brush.

NARCISSI & TULIPS - Using Narcissi and Tulips

To give tulips an exotic, lily-like appearance try opening out their petals so they can turn back on themselves; such petals are called 'reflexed'. Very gently curl each petal backwards between your finger and thumb, repeating the process until it retains a graceful line. Narcissi come with a natural paper like cover over the flower buds. To remove them, carefully pull down the protective cover and, using a sharp knife, cut it off neatly where it joins the stalk.

STOCKS - Buying and Conditioning

Stocks tend to be difficult flowers to deal with and have a short life span in vase arrangements and have weak stems. Careful conditioning can overcome these problems.

1. Remove the lower white section of the stems, along with the excess foliage. Once arranged, the stems should be recut often to keep them fresh.

2. Keep away from direct sunlight, heat and drafts.

WILD FLOWERS - Wild Flower Tips

1. If you pick flowers in the wild, try to give them a drink of water as soon as possible. Wrap the stems in damp tissues and put them in water immediately.

2. To have access to your own personal wild flower garden, look for wild flower mixtures in specialty seed catalogs. There are wildflower garden mixtures to attract birds and butterflies; a flowering lawn mix, and coastal woodland mixtures suitable for specific regions and soil types.

TECHNIQUES
Dried Flowers

Dried flowers are commercially available through specialty flower shops and a number of craft and variety stores. Due to improved techniques for preserving flowers, today the selection has broadened to encompass everything from exotic pods to nostalgic, Victorian nosegays flowers. The basic technique remains the same, the fresh flowers are cut, banded and hung upside- down to dry in a warm, well ventilated area. The newest additions to the process are custom dying flowers in decorator colors and dipping in glycerin to add flexibility to the naturally brittle flowers. Not all flowers are conducive but these techniques have expanded the selections and longevity of many flowers. As mentioned in a previous chapter, we recommend strengthening weak, dried, stems with the use of floral wire and floral tape. The real plus when working with dried flowers is the fact that they are completely reusable and can be recycled to work with fresh and silk flowers, especially dried "filler" flowers such as baby's breath and statice.

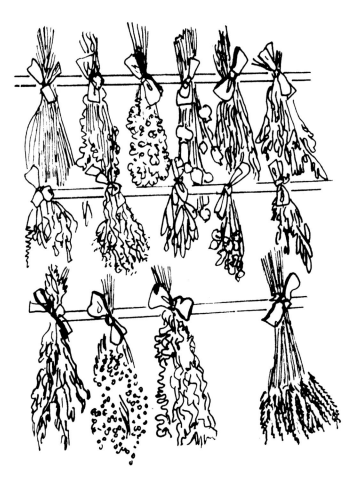

TECHNIQUES
Silk Flowers

Silk flowers are available in various ranges of price and quality. The care and handling to create life-like flowers is the same regardless of the quality. Here are a few hints to make your silks look like real flowers.

1. Newly purchased or stored silk flowers are often smashed or flattened from being tightly packed in boxes. To revive these flowers we suggest two options, the first is to carefully manipulate the petals and leaves by hand, smoothing and twisting the flower and straightening the stems. The second idea is to gently steam the flowers over a tea kettle or use a portable, hand held steamer. The trick is to steam lightly. Do not allow the flower to absorb too much steam or it will become wet and the colors may run. When steamed properly, the wrinkles will fall out and the blossoms will regain their original shape. You may wish to hand manipulate the steamed blossom if there are special shapes to be attained.

2. Inexpensive silk flowers are often sold in clusters which can be separated into individual stems to allow more flexibility in styling.

3. To add a touch of glamour for a special occasion, silks can be sprayed with aerosol glitter which can be found at your favorite craft shop or variety store. Stylists refer to this product as "floral sparkle spray".

4. Silk flowers are reusable and will last forever if properly cared for. To freshen the silks you can spray the flowers with regular leaf shine which can be purchased in the garden department of most hardware and variety stores.

5. To stretch the uses of your silk flowers we suggest mixing them with fresh or dried flowers.

TECHNIQUES
Food Preparation

Techniques for food preparation are almost identical to regular meal preparation, except there is more precision with regard to cutting the greens the same length for the vases. Any fresh fruits that normally brown or oxidize with air, should be dipped in citric acid or the juice of an orange or lemon. Fruits and vegetables that are susceptible to shriveling or drying out should be soaked in ice water before displaying in the arrangement. Carrot sticks, radishes, celery etc. all have a tendency to go limp or shrivel up as their natural moisture evaporates. When soaked, they stay fresh for hours. When serving cream based dips and sauces, we suggest you display the sauce or dip in a smaller bowl nestled in a larger bowl of ice, this will allow the dip to remain fresh for hours. To create a truly festive look to your hors d'oeuvres do not forget to add a few fresh flowers to brighten the presentation. A good example of this idea is illustrated with our salsa and chip arrangement which is colorfully accented with red carnations against green parsley.

If you would like to add a few new tools to your kitchen repertoire, we would like to suggest that you invest in a garnishing kit. Once you become familiar with these tools you can carve flowers from fruits and vegetables and add a professional touch to your food presentation. Guaranteed to impress any guest.

JANUARY

NEW YEARS'

FEBRUARY

VALENTINE'S DAY

MARCH

ST. PATRICK'S DAY

APRIL

EASTER

MAY

MOTHER'S DAY

JUNE

FATHER'S DAY

JULY

INDEPENDENCE DAY

AUGUST

WEDDINGS

SEPTEMBER

BIRTHDAYS

OCTOBER

HALLOWEEN

NOVEMBER

THANKSGIVING

DECEMBER

CHRISTMAS

Special Occasions & Holidays

JANUARY

The best way to start the New Year is with an attractive centerpiece. Whether you choose an informal arrangement of finger foods for the ball game or a dramatic, elegant centerpiece to ring in the New Year, we have got what you are looking for!

NEW YEAR'S

Fresh:

White mini carnations, red anemones and green leather fern are the basic ingredients for this simple, yet stunning arrangement, accented with silver mylar curling ribbon.

1. Fill the Floral Design and Floral Seven vases with fresh water.
2. Cut your flower stems to nine inches.
3. Place the glass disc in the center of the Floral Design and add the Floral Seven on top.
4. Fill the vases with two -three stems of each flower, alternating the red and white as shown in the photo.
5. Add the leather fern at random to contrast the flowers and fill in the open spaces.
6. Position your Floral Design at the desired location.

Silk:

This simple arrangement can be styled with silk flowers (as seen) or can be done with live cuttings which will eventually root if the vases are filled with water. For this example, we have used silk variegated pothos and magenta, silk spider mums. The holiday accent is a mylar, star garland which we have twisted into the arrangement.

1. Fill the Floral Design with silica sand, using a funnel for convenience.

2. Fill each vase with a seven inch trailing section of pothos.

3. Add one six inch stem of spider mum, placing one in every third vase.

4. Twist the garland to create large random loops and place in the center of the arrangement.

5. For variety you can place a four inch potted plant in the center or add the glass platform disc and use a large candle or figurine as the focal point.

Dried:

Silver poinsettias, black chrysanthemums and grey, silk baby's breath are the elements which make up this unique, elegant centerpiece. We have taken a variety of dried grasses, leaves and flowers, and sprayed them with metallic floral paint to give them richness. The other floral element is a black silk chrysanthemum. To add festivity to this arrangement we used silver and black serpentines and nestled the arrangement in copper, mylar party shreds.

1. Fill the Floral Design and the Floral Seven with silica sand or salt.
2. Cut the flower stems to nine inches.
3. Place the glass disc in the center of the Floral Design and position the Floral Seven on top.
4. Place two -three stems of "filler" flowers in each vase.
5. Alternately place your silk accent flowers. Use one flower for every three vases, until you have even coverage. Be sure to accent light against dark to create the most contrast.
6. Position your Floral Design at the desired location.
7. Surround the base of the arrangement with copper party shreds.
8. Toss a few serpentines and drape from the flowers onto the tabletop.

Food:

The beautiful color and flavor of fresh shrimp, cheese and black olives make this appetizer a welcome centerpiece for any gathering, we have also added a delicious cocktail sauce for variety. The shrimp and cheese cubes are threaded onto bamboo skewers which are secured in a whole cabbage, and garnished with fresh parsley.

1. Fill the vases of the Floral Design with fresh water.

2. Cut the parsley at four inch lengths and fill each vase with three to four stems of parsley. Use as much as needed to create a solid field of parsley in the vases.

3. Place a small head of cabbage in the center of the Floral Design. We have used green cabbage but purple looks equally good. Do not use the glass platform.

4. Make up twelve individual skewers using cubes of your favorite cheeses, olives, and shrimps. Alternate the items as you thread them onto the skewers.

5. Hollow the cabbage top to accommodate the cocktail sauce.

6. Secure the skewers in the cabbage. (You may wish to use an ice pick or metal cake tester to make the holes for the bamboo skewers if the cabbage is too dense to penetrate easily.)

7. Garnish with a fresh parsley sprig.

FEBRUARY

Whether you choose to make these arrangements as gifts or accent your own surroundings, each selection we have created conveys the same theme: romance.

VALENTINE'S DAY

Fresh:

Every shade of red and pink are featured in this heart-stopping bouquet. Our reds and pinks are created from tulips, heather, and mini carnations. To contrast the red tones we are using white cushion chrysanthemums and to add a special theme accent we have used a variety of heart shaped picks to convey the Valentine sentiment.

1. Fill the Floral Design and Floral Seven with fresh water.
2. Cut all the flower stems at six inches.
3. Place the glass disc in the center of the Floral Design and add the Floral Seven on top.
4. Alternate red carnations and white mums using one to two stems of contrasting flowers in each vase until the bouquet looks full.
5. Add one stem of heather to each vase until the arrangement is filled evenly.
6. Position the Floral Design at the desired location .

Silk:

Love birds are the focal point in this fresh looking silk bouquet featuring pale pink azaleas and dark green leather fern.

1. Fill the Floral Design with silica sand or grits.
2. Clip your flower stems to six inches.
3. Place one azalea stem and one fern stems in each vase. Add more ferns where necessary to create even distribution.
4. Position your Floral Design at the desired location.
5. Place the glass disc in the center of the Floral Design.
6. Place the ceramic doves in the center of the Floral Design.

Dried:

It is hard to believe this beautiful arrangement is one of the easiest and quickest to assemble. We have only two elements to deal with; dried baby's breath and freeze dried roses. (Look for long stemmed, full sprays of baby's breath and long stemmed roses)

1. Fill the Floral Design and Floral Seven vases with grits, using a funnel. Style the two vases separately.

2. Cut the flower stems at nine inches.

3. Add one beautiful rose surrounded with three to four stems of baby's breath, creating mini bouquets. Fill every vase with a mini bouquet.

4. Position the Floral Design at the desired location.

5. Add the glass disc to the center of the Floral Design.

6. Carefully place the Floral Seven in the center of the Floral Design.

Food:

One box of foil covered bon bons adds a special touch to this edible arrangement. The floral elements can be fresh or silk depending on your preference. We have shown fresh pothos cuttings which are accented with red ribbon bows and a few stems of baby's breath.

1. Fill the Floral Design with fresh water (or silica sand if using silk).
2. Cut the pothos vines at five inches.
3. Fill each vase with two to three pothos vines depending on the fullness of the leaves and vines.
4. Wire three inch (diameter) ribbon bows onto picks, six to eight bows will cover nicely.
5. Carefully pierce the bon bons onto round toothpicks, using one toothpick per candy and piercing only the bottom layer of chocolate. (this avoids excessive seepage*)
6. Insert the toothpicks in the vases, alternating with the ribbon bows.
7. Position the Floral Design at the desired location.
8. Add the glass disc to the center of the Floral Design.
9. Place a half head of purple cabbage on platform and secure twenty four toothpicked bon bons into the cabbage.

* Place the bon bons which are to be skewered in the refrigerator or freezer for easier handling.

MARCH

You don't have to be Irish to enjoy these beautiful centerpieces. Our variety of floral elements reflect the colors of early spring and the gaiety of St. Patrick's Day.

ST. PATRICK'S DAY

Fresh:
Classic white daisies and fresh green eucalyptus are accented with three leprechaun pipes and a wee green bowler hat. The emerald green water in the vases is achieved with food coloring and dyed green moss is used as an accent to the arrangement.

1. Fill a quart bottle with fresh water and add a few drops of green food coloring until you achieve the shade of green you desire.
2. Fill the vases with colored water.
3. Stack the Floral Seven on top of the Floral Design using the glass disc as a platform.
4. Cut your flower stems to seven inches.
5. Add the eucalyptus to each vase and fill until there is even distribution and the arrangement looks balanced.
6. Place one daisy stem in each vase.
7. Accent with the pipes and bowler hat in the top third of the arrangement.
8. Use decorative green moss to soften the base and add richness to the display.

Silk:

The Floral Seven is the basis for this smaller scaled arrangement featuring white silk camellias and a tall, tapered candle as a focal point. The novelty accents are Irish leprechaun pipes.

1. Fill the Floral Seven with grits.

2. Cut the silk flowers to five inches, using wire cutters.

3. Carefully smooth the flower leaves between the index finger and thumb to create a realistic, life-like effect.

4. Place one flower in six vases leaving the top vase empty.

5. Secure a tall, white or green tapered candle in the center vase and accent with two pipes.

Dried:

Yellow yarrow, purple statice, green mini gyp, natural baby's breath and mini silver dollars are the dried materials we have used for this lovely arrangement. The subtle suggestion of St. Patricks's Day is achieved with a traditional shamrock which tops the bouquet.

1. Fill the Floral Design and the Floral Seven with grits using the funnel for convenience.
2. Cut the flower stems at seven inches.
3. Make mini bouquets by combining one stem of each flower and place one bunch in each vase.
4. Fill the "holes" or gaps in the arrangement with baby's breath until the bouquet looks complete.

Food:

The emerald green of Ireland is created with fresh parsley and green ribbon bows (wired onto toothpicks) which become a perfect backdrop for white daisies. The cracker spread is cream cheese topped with a delicious coating of green jalapeno jelly.

1. Fill the Floral Design with fresh water.

2. Cut the parsley to four inches.

3. Cut twelve daisies to five inches.

4. Fill the vases with parsley until there is even coverage without gaps or holes.

5. Place three daisies in two opposite points of the top tier of vases.

6. Alternate the remaining daisies on the lower tier, two per vase.

7. Place the five ribbon bows in the negative spaces between the daisies.

8. Place a shallow, six inch glass bowl in the center of the Floral Design.

9. Center an eight ounce brick of cream cheese in the bowl and top with a half cup of green jalapeno jelly.

10. Surround the cream cheese with your favorite crackers and serve!

APRIL

Easter is more than a holiday, it is the celebration of spring, and flowers are the most beautiful way to express this special time.

EASTER

Fresh:

We have styled this mixed bouquet with white daisies, purple liatrus, purple tulips, red carnations, yellow freesias and baby's breath. The bright colors and high contrast truly says spring!

1. Fill the Floral Design and Floral Seven vases with fresh water.
2. Place Floral Seven on Floral Design using glass disc as platform.
3. Cut flower stems at six inches.
4. Place one tulip and one liatrus in every other vase of the Floral Seven and every third vase of the Floral Design.
5. Fill remaining vases with alternated flower selections.

Silk:

White lilies, magenta lilies, yellow roses, and magenta mums are used to create this traditional spring bouquet. The complete arrangement stands about twenty four inches tall.

1. Fill the Floral Design and Floral Seven vases with grits using a funnel.
2. Cut the stems to seven inches.
3. Place Floral Seven on Floral Design using glass disc as platform.
4. Place one yellow rose in the top vase and one in every other vase of the Floral Seven, and every third vase of the Floral Design.
5. Combine one of each remaining flower and add to vases until full.

Dried:

The combination of silk and dried flowers are exhibited in this darling design. Our creation features, silk pothos, silk violets and dried baby's breath, accented with a ceramic bunny nestled in straw, complete with Easter eggs.

1. Fill the Floral Design with grits using a funnel.

2. Cut the silk pothos vines to six inches.

3. Clip the violets and baby's breath to six inches.

4. Place three to four stems of pothos in each vase.

5. Combine one violet stem with three stems of baby's breath and place one in every third vase.

6. Position the Floral Design at the desired location.

7. Add the glass disc to the center of the Floral Design.

8. Place the ceramic bunny figurine on the glass disc.

9. Surround the base of the Floral Design with straw to create a nest. (Sterilized straw is available at craft and variety stores)

10. Add a few dyed Easter eggs to the nest to complete the theme.

Food:

The brilliant color contrast of emerald green parsley and magenta sweet peas are a perfect backdrop for the delicious spinach dip; served in a hollowed, round loaf of sourdough bread.

1. Fill the Floral Design with fresh water.

2. Cut the parsley at four inches and the sweet peas at five inches.

3. Fill each vase with three to four stems of parsley or until the vase looks full and evenly covered.

4. Place one sweet pea stem in every third vase until there is an even scattering of blossoms.

5. Position the Floral Design at the desired location.

6. Carefully cut a five inch circular slice off the top of a six inch loaf of sourdough bread. Scoop out the soft bread inside to make a bowl from the bread shell.*

7. Fill the empty bread shell with a thick spread or dip. We have used our favorite spinach dip for this example.

8. Garnish with a beautiful sweet pea blossom.

* If the dip or spread you are using is too watery, simply hide a small bowl in the bread shell to prevent the bread from softening.

MAY

Beautiful flowers arranged and accented with significant mementos are sure to please the Mother in your life. We have styled four unique bouquets to make her day special.

MOTHER'S DAY

Fresh:

Bold, pink Gerbera daisies, delicate baby's breath and leather fern are combined in our Floral Design and highlighted with an elegant, white candle.

1. Fill the Floral Design with fresh water.
2. Cut the flower and fern stems at seven inches.
3. Place one daisy stem in each vase with two ferns and two baby's breath stems. (We suggest wiring the daisy stems before incorporating them in the arrangement because they have a tendency to droop).
4. Fill all the vases and add more baby's breath if there are any gaps or visible "holes".
5. Position the Floral Design at the desired location.
6. Add the glass disc to the center of the Floral Design.
7. Place the candle on the glass disc.

Silk:

One of our favorite, truly feminine arrangements is created with peach hyacinth, pale pink peonies, and pink azaleas .Unlike all the other arrangements, we are using two lengths because we want the spiked look of the hyacinth for contrast.

1. Fill the Floral Design and Floral Seven with grits, using a funnel.
2. Place Floral Seven on Floral Design using glass disc as platform.
3. Clip the peonies at eight inches and the hyacinth at ten inches.
4. Start with one hyacinth and one peony and place in center of the Floral Seven.
5. Create eight more of this combination and place three more on the lower tier of the Floral Seven and the remaining five equally balanced in the Floral Design.
6. Fill the remaining vases with one each, of the azalea and peony combination.

Dried:

Nostalgia and romance are created with freeze dried roses, mauve heather, dried statice and lavender bows for accent.

1. Fill the Floral Design and Floral Seven with grits using a funnel.

2. Cut the flower stems at seven inches.

3. Place the glass disc in the center of the Floral Design and position the Floral Seven on top.

4. Fill the vases with two to three stems of heather and statice, these are considered filler flowers.

5. Add one freeze dried rose flower to every third vase.

6. Add one lavender bow to every alternate third vase.

7. Position the Floral Design at the desired location.

Food:

We absolutely love this centerpiece and always get rave reviews whenever we present it. Because it is colorful and feminine we have selected it as our Mother's Day feature. We have used parsley, pink waxflower and fruit kabobs made of grapes, cantaloupe, strawberries and kumquats.

1. Fill the Floral Design with fresh water.
2. Cut the parsley at four inches and the waxflower at five inches.
3. Fill the vases with three stems of parsley and one stem of wax flower.
4. Make twelve fruit kabobs by threading your favorite fruit onto six inchbamboo skewers. We have chosen grapes, cantaloupe, strawberries and kumquats because of their beautiful color and flavor, and because they hold up well at room temperature.
5. Position the Floral Design at the desired location.
6. Remove glass platform.
7. Place a small head of green cabbage in the center of the Floral Design.
8. Insert the skewers of fruit kabobs in the cabbage head.*

* Option: Arrange the skewers around the perimeter of the cabbage and hollow out the center of the cabbage and fill with your favorite fruit dip, sauce or topping.

JUNE

You may not have considered flowers as a manly way to accent Father's Day, but our stylist has proven that flowers work for all occasions!

FATHER'S DAY

Fresh:

This arrangement is so rich and strong with color that it will easily complement that special Father's Day dinner or brunch. We have used magenta spider mums, Queen Annes lace, blue delphiniums, white delphiniums, pink wax-flower and rosey, peach alstromeria.

1. Fill the Floral Design and Floral Seven with fresh water.
2. Place Floral Seven on Floral Design using glass disc as platform.
3. Cut the flower stems at ten inches.
4. Place two to three unlike flowers in each vase depending on the size of the stems. (You may have to pare the stems with a knife if they are too thick).
5. Use the white Queen Annes lace as a filler for the holes and spaces that are left after arranging your colored flowers.

Silk:

The beautiful textures in this arrangement are created from a mixture of silk and dried materials. We have even used mixed bird seed to fill the vases with extra visual texture. Our plant materials are: dried, blue statice sinuata, rust, silk chrysanthemums, brown mini silver dollars, rust "bamboo" eucalyptus, mini cattails and white bleached yarrow. The entire arrangement is encircled in a rust, twelve inch, twig wreath .

1. Using a funnel, fill the Floral Design and Floral Seven with wild bird seed.
2. Place Floral Seven on Floral Design using glass disc as platform.
3. Cut the flower stems at ten inches.
4. Fill the vases with three stems of dried materials, alternating the content.
5. Place thirteen silk chrysanthemums in every two vases until there is random coverage.
6. Center the arrangement in the twig wreath.

Dried:

We have selected a ceramic duck as the focal point for this clever arrangement created with natural green "silver dollar" eucalyptus and rust "bamboo" eucalyptus for color and textural contrast.

1. Fill the Floral Design with grits using a funnel.
2. Cut the dried flower stems at nine inches.
3. Place one to three stems of the green "silver dollar" eucalyptus in each vase.
4. Add an accent stem of rust eucalyptus to every other vase.
5. Position the Floral Design at the desired location.
6. Add the glass disc to the center of the Floral Design.
7. Place the ceramic duck on the glass disc.

Optional: Place small stems of rust eucalyptus to create a nest effect if there is room on the glass platform.

Food:

Perfect for appetizers at a dinner party or casual enough to serve for the "boys night" of cards or the ball game. We have skewered hearty snack food items like salami and an assortment of cheeses and presented it on a head of cabbage surrounded with fresh parsley.

1. Fill the vases in the Floral Design with fresh water.

2. Cut the parsley stems at four inches.

3. Using six inch bamboo skewers, thread an assortment of your favorite meats and cheeses to create twelve kabobs. We have shown six cheese kabobs made with Swiss, Cheddar and Jalapeno Jack cheese cubes, and six meat kabobs made with hard salami, summer sausage, pepperoni and cherry tomatoes.

4. Fill each glass vase with fresh parsley.

5. Remove the glass platform.

6. Place the head of red cabbage in the center of the Floral Design.

7. Secure the skewers in the cabbage, alternating the cheese and meat kabobs.

8. Add a kabob skewer to every third vase of parsley.

JULY

The Fourth of July is the official kickoff for summer, and a great excuse for a holiday gathering. The selections we have created for you will accent a picnic table as well as a dinner table. They are fun and patriotic. We even added a theatrical touch with real sparklers which are sure to be the center of attention!

INDEPENDENCE DAY

Fresh:

Our star spangled arrangement is made with baby's breath, ivory colored spider mums, red carnations, and blue iris. To guarantee everyone's attention, we have inserted real sparklers to light up the evening and accented the flowers with a silvery star garland.

1. Fill the Floral Design and Floral Seven vases with fresh water.
2. Place Floral Seven on Floral Design using glass disc as platform.
3. Cut the flower stems at nine inches.
4. Place one of each flower in every vase, alternating to create variety in placement.
5. Insert six to eight sparklers* at random, reserving one for the center vase at the top of the arrangement.
6. Twist twenty-four inches of star garland throughout the arrangement.*

*Place the arrangement in a safe, non-combustable area before lighting the sparklers!

Silk:

The high contrast of red, white and blue accented with four American flags has a real Americana look. We have used red carnations, white impatience, and blue roses as our floral elements. The flags are novelty size, about two inches by three inches.

1. Using a funnel, fill the Floral Design and Floral Seven with grits.

2. Place Floral Seven on Floral Design using glass disc as platform.

3. Cut the flower stems at ten inches.

4. Combine the white impatience, blue roses and red carnations, placing one of each in every vase.

5. Accent the arrangement with three American flags, one on top and two on the sides.

Dried:

Freeze dried plant elements are featured in this bouquet. We have used pothos, red mini carnations and blue baby's breath with a beautiful white candle as the focal point for our patriotic presentation.

1. Using a funnel, fill the Floral Design and Floral Seven with grits.
2. Clip the pothos to seven inch lengths and clip the flower stems at six inches.
3. Combine two pothos vines, one carnation and two stems of baby's breath and place in each vase.
4. Position the Floral Design at the desired location.
5. Add the glass disc to the center of the Floral Design.
6. Place the candle in the center of the glass disc.

Food:

We feel that this is one of the most festive and creative centerpieces we have designed. We have an explosion of vegetables starting with skewers of cherry tomatoes, mushrooms, olives and individual celery, carrot and green onion sticks which are nestled in parsley. The candle is cleverly placed in a hollowed artichoke which is sitting in a hollowed head of cabbage.

1. Fill the Floral Design with fresh water.

2. Cut the parsley stems at four inches and fill the vases with cut parsley.

3. Thread the cherry tomatoes, mushrooms and olives onto six inch bamboo skewers, until there are six kabobs.

4. Cut a round circle four inches in diameter and hollow the domed portion of the cabbage to accommodate an artichoke.

5. Insert the artichoke in the cabbage.

6. Place the hollowed head of cabbage in the center of the Floral Design.

7. Add a two inches candle to the center of the artichoke. (You may need to remove a few leaves from the center of the artichoke in order to accommodate the candle.)

8. Secure the bamboo skewers in the cabbage head, working around the artichoke.

9. Spear individual olives and radishes onto toothpicks and secure in the negative spaces on the cabbage.

AUGUST

The cost of hosting a wedding can be quite expensive when professional services are used for all the details. We are happy to present some beautiful, impressive arrangements that can be made with your Floral Design at almost half the cost of a florist. These designs are suitable for banquet tables, church alters or reception areas. We have done our wedding arrangements with fresh flowers, silk flowers, dried flowers and a special food arrangement perfect for your reception!

ROMANTIC WEDDING CENTERPIECES

Fresh:

Nothing looks more romantic than a heavenly bouquet of fresh baby's breath and pink carnations.

1. The stems are cut fourteen inches long. (You may need to wire the carnations if the stems are too weak. Another hint when dealing with carnations; gently open the petals by rolling the flower in the palm of your hand. Use twenty four carnations.)

2. Fill the vases with fresh water.

3. Due to the size of the arrangement, style each vase separately.

4. Surround each carnation stem with three lush, thirteen inch stem baby's breath and place each cluster in a vase. You can determine how full the arrangement will be after filling two to three vases. If it seems too skimpy add more baby's breath and repeat with all the vases. It is difficult to give exact quantities because the fullness and quality of the flowers vary.

5. Place the glass disc in the center of the Floral Design and add the Floral Seven after the vase has been placed in its final location.

6. We have surrounded the arrangement with bridal tulle for a romantic, cloud-like effect. This looks especially beautiful as a centerpiece for the bridal table.

7. The completed arrangement stands about twenty- four inches tall. If you desire a smaller arrangement, cut the stems shorter.

Silk:

The elegant look of a fresh arrangement has been created with white silk camellias, pink silk spider mums.

1. Clip the stems at ten inches.
2. Using a funnel for convenience, fill the vases with salt (add rice in humid climates to prevent the salt from compacting).
3. Place the glass disc in the center of the Floral Design and add the Floral Seven.
4. Arrange the flowers using one spider mum for every two camellias.
5. Repeat until all the vases are filled.

Dried:

To accent a wedding theme of nostalgia, we have designed a Victorian arrangement featuring: dried mini flame roses, natural preserved baby's breath, dried pink heather and preserved leather leaf fern.

1. Cut the flower stems at five inches.
2. Fill the Floral Design vases with white grits.
3. Surround the rose stem with two stems of baby's breath and heather and place in every other vase. Fill the remaining vases with the baby's breath and heather. Add the leather fern to the lower tier of vases using one or two stems per vase depending on the fullness of the fern.
4. Place the glass disc in the center of the Floral Design.
5. Use a wedding cake topper as the centerpiece and place on the glass disc.

Food:

The simplicity of chips and dip becomes a striking centerpiece when presented in the Floral Design. We have combined fresh fuchsia colored sweet williams, ivory spider mums and fresh, emerald colored parsley! The chips are large ruffle style potato chips and the dip is a classic sour cream and onion dip.

1. Cut the flower stems to match the longest overall length of parsley stem. This usually does not exceed six to seven inches.

2. Fill the vases on the Floral Design with fresh water.

3. Fill each vase with a cluster of parsley and alternate one of each flower stem in every third vase until they are evenly distributed.

4. Place the arrangement at the desired location.

5. Add the glass disc to the center of the Floral Design.

6. Center a large glass chip and dip bowl which has already been filled with chips and dip.

7. Garnish the dip with a large sprig of parsley and a stem of sweet william.

SEPTEMBER

The most frequent special occasion that we celebrate has to be birthdays! With the aid of the Floral Design you will have the flexibility to style light-hearted, juvenile arrangements for the kids in your life as well as sophisticated, elegant bouquets for the not-so-young kids in your life. You are only limited by your imagination.

MEMORABLE BIRTHDAYS

Fresh:

The high contrast of these colors creates a festive mood perfect for any birthday celebration. The fresh flowers we have selected for this bouquet are: pale yellow chrysanthemums, bright yellow daisies, purple statice, red carnations, and green leather fern.

1. Cut all the flower stems at eight inches.
2. Stack the Floral Seven on the Floral Design using the glass platform.
3. Fill the vases with fresh water.
4. Start with one flower group at a time, i.e. carnations, and place one in every third vase. Arrange both vases using this technique.
5. Continue this technique until all the flowers have been alternately arranged in the vases. (Due to the number of individual flowers in the bouquet, there will be more than one flower in every vase.)
6. After all the flowers are distributed, and the vases have been combined, add the leather leaf fern throughout the bouquet.
7. Add the large clown party favor to the center of the bouquet. (Use a pick if the favor is on a short stem)
8. Next add four smaller party favors to the center of the bouquet. Use two on each side if it is to be viewed as a free standing centerpiece.
9. Finally attach two balloons to the top to accent the large clown, the focal point of the arrangement.

   (If you need to move or re-position the arrangement, remember to separate the top unit before moving to avoid spilling.)

Silk:

The beautiful color contrast in this arrangement is from: yellow roses, white dogwood, purple chrysanthemum with attached green leaves.

1. Clip your flower stems with wire cutters at seven inches.

2. Fill the vases with "grits". (Use a funnel to pour the grits easily).

3. Add the glass disc to the center of the Floral Design and place the Floral Seven on top.

4. Start with one flower group at a time, i.e. yellow roses, and place one in every other vase on the Floral Seven and one in every third vase on the Floral Design. Continue this technique until all the flowers have been alternately arranged in the vases. (Due to the number of individual flowers in the bouquet, there will be more than one flower in each vase).

5. Insert eighteen to twenty opalescent purple balloon picks throughout the arrangement or substitute another purple or hot pink party favor.

6. Place the completed arrangement on a bed of iridescent cellophane shreds and insert the pink noise maker favors as a festive accent.

Dried:

Texture is the key word in this arrangement. We have combined natural dried pink heather, purple thistles, white ting ting, dyed blue baby's breath and yellow silk daisies.

1. Cut all the flower stems at eight inches.
2. Fill the vases with white silica sand using a funnel for convenience.
3. Place the glass disc in the center of the Floral Design and add the Floral Seven.
4. Start with one flower group at a time, and place one flower in every other vase. Continue this technique until all the flowers have been arranged in alternating vases.
5. As a focal point, theme element, we have used an inflated, mylar balloon pick with a birthday greeting in the center of the arrangement.

Food:

We have created a special "double duty" birthday treat by combining the birthday cake with a floral arrangement. The centerpiece for this special birthday presentation is a seven inch frosted cake nestled in a ring of yellow daisies, white chrysanthemum, red carnations, baby's breath and green ivy cuttings.

1. Cut all your flower stems at eight inches.

2. Fill the large ring of vases with water.

3. Start with one flower group at a time, and place one in every other vase. Continue this technique until all the flowers have been arranged in alternate vases. The cut ivy should be treated as a flower element. (Due to the number of individual flowers in the bouquet, there will be more than one flower in every vase.)

4. Place the glass disc in the center of the vase, creating a platform for your cake.

5. The Happy Birthday banner is placed in the center of the cake and is accented with blue, red and yellow ribbon curls.

6. As a final touch, a cascade of red carnations, yellow daisies and white mums are gently placed on the cake by inserting a short two inch stem into the frosting.

* The cake pictured is a yellow cake with chocolate and vanilla frosting, garnished with multicolored cake sprinkles around the base and on the top.

OCTOBER

The beautiful colors of autumn brighten the gray days of fall, especially if they have been captured in exciting bouquets and clever centerpieces. Our stylist has combined some rich colors and great textures in the next four arrangements that are as easy as they are beautiful.

HALLOWEEN

Fresh:

Purple chrysanthemums, yellow freesia, purple liatrus, mini gyp and rust alstromeria make up this jewel tone bouquet. The colors and richness of the flowers make it suitable for royalty.

1. Fill the Floral Design and Floral Seven with fresh water.
2. Place Floral Seven on Floral Design using glass disc as platform.
3. Cut the flower stems at nine inches.
4. Combine the chrysanthemums and freesia and place in every vase.
5. Place the liatrus in the top and every other vase of the Floral Seven, and every third vase of the Floral Design.
6. Alternate the alstromeria in every three vases, and use the mini gyp as a filler to accent the overall arrangement.

Silk:

This blaze of color is probably the easiest and most striking of all our arrangements. We have filled the vases with water to give the illusion of fresh flowers, and used rust silk alstromerias for that fiery color. When purchasing silk alstromerias look for multiple blossoms on each stem which can be separated and used individually.

1. Fill the Floral Design and Floral Seven with fresh water.

2. Clip the flower stems at seven inches.

3. Dip the flower stems in clear polish to seal the metal and prevent rusting.

4. Place three stems in each vase.

5. Position the Floral Design at the desired location.

6. Add the glass disc to the center of the Floral Design.

7. Place the Floral Seven on the glass disc.

Dried:

Who can resist the charm of this whimsical scarecrow sitting in his own mini pumpkin patch. This arrangement uses ivy cutting that will continue to grow as long there is water in your vases, making this a year round background for almost any clever focal point elements. To complete this holiday favorite we have surrounded the base of the Floral Design with hay and used a few preserved maple leaves for a splash of color.

1. Fill the Floral Design with fresh water.

2. Use ivy cuttings that are four to six inches long.

3. Place two to three ivy cuttings in each vase depending on the fullness of the cuttings.

4. Position the Floral Design at the desired location.

5. Add the glass disc to the center of the Floral Design.

6. Center your scarecrow on the glass disc and add a little hay to disguise the glass.

7. Secure the pumpkins novelties* onto wooden picks and place in every third vase.

8. Surround the base of the arrangement with hay and add a few preserved maple leaves for a color accent.

*The pumpkins are available as floral pick accessories in most craft supply and variety stores.

64

Food:

Trick or treat candy is always tempting but we have also made it the center of attention in our Halloween food arrangement by surrounding it with pothos and bright orange bows.

1. Fill the Floral Design with silica sand.

2. Cut the pothos vines at six inches.

3. Place two or three stems of pothos in each vase depending on the fullness of the vines.

4. Place the Floral Design at the desired location.

5. Add the glass disc to the center of the Floral Design.

6. Place a shallow, clear glass bowl in the center of the glass disc and fill with an assortment of your favorite candies.

7. Accent the arrangement with orange ribbon bows which have been wired to picks.

NOVEMBER

The splendor of a Thanksgiving table will be enhanced with one of our impressive arrangements. The Floral Design is easy and fast to use. Creating a special arrangement will not burden the host or chef (in case it happens to be one and the same) and will bring rave reviews to rival the turkey!

THANKSGIVING

Fresh:
A traditional mixed bouquet has been created with yellow daisies, rust alstromerias, purple statice, dried wheat and accented with Indian corn.

1. Fill the Floral Design with fresh water.

2. Cut the flower stems at nine inches (If this is to be used as a centerpiece at the dinner table, gauge the size of this arrangement by the available space at the dinner table. You may wish to condense the flowers by cutting shorter stems)

3. Place the glass disc in the center of the Floral Design and position the Floral Seven on top.

4. Combine one alstromeria, daisy and statice and place one bunch in each vase.

5. Fill the negative spaces or holes with additional statice until the arrangement looks full and evenly balanced.

6. Place one wheat straw in the top vase of the Floral Seven, and every third vase of the Floral Design.

7. Accent the arrangement with Indian corn or ornamental gourds.

Silk:

Silk flowers never looked so realistic and fresh! Traditional fall colors are the key to this simple and airy arrangement. The silk selections we have chosen are flame ranuculus, pale yellow baby's breath and emerald green, Maiden Hair fern.

1. Fill the Floral Design and Floral Seven with silica sand.
2. Place the Floral Seven on top of the Floral Design using the glass disc as a platform.
3. Clip the stems at seven inches.
4. Place one or two ranuculus in each vase.
5. Fill the negative spaces or holes with additional statice until the arrangement looks full and evenly balanced.
6. Add two stems of baby's breath and one stem of fern in each vase. The end result should be light and airy in appearance.

Dried:

Preserved flowers and leaves are the newest in dried floral materials. To create this arrangement we have selected preserved maple leaves because we love the rich color, and accents of purple statice. To add a whimsical touch we have incorporated colorful, green ting ting that seem to tease the ceramic kitten.

1. Fill the Floral Design with silica sand.
2. Use long stemmed maple leaves, or wire the leaves to floral picks if the stems are too short to sit securely in the vases.
3. Use two or three leaves per vase.
4. Position the Floral Design at the desired location.
5. Add the glass disc to the center of the Floral Design.
6. Place the ting ting in every third vase, alternate the spacing to achieve even distribution.
7. Accent with delicate stems of purple statice in every third vase.
8. Place the ceramic kitten in the center of the glass disc.

Food:

Carrot salad never looked so appealing! Rather than creating an appetizer, we thought you should see how beautifully the Floral Design works with a buffet selection. The bright green parsley has been accented with carrot sticks and wheat which conveys the harvest theme of Thanksgiving.

1. Fill the Floral Design with fresh water.

2. Peel and slice two carrots and make carrots sticks about six inches long.

3. Cut the parsley stems at four inches.

4. Fill the vases with two or three sprigs of parsley per vase.

5. Insert one carrot stick in every other vase.

6. Insert one stem of wheat in every empty vase.

7. Position the Floral Design at the desired location.

8. Add the glass disc to the center of the Floral Design.

9. Place a glass bowl containing carrot salad onto the glass disc and garnish with a sprig of parsley.

DECEMBER

Uses for the Floral Design during the holidays are endless. We have combined natural greens, flowers and festive ornaments to create these bouquets.

CHRISTMAS/HANUKKAH

Fresh:

Perfect for that special dinner table or buffet, our combination of white spider mums, red ribbon bows and bright green leather fern is sure to garner compliments from your guests. For a unique twist on candles, we have used clear, kerosene candles that add a touch of elegance to the table.

1. Fill the Floral Design with fresh water.

2. Cut the flower stems at nine inches.

3. Fill each vase with two or three stems of spider mums.

4. Wire four large red ribbon bows approximately three inches in diameter to floral picks.

5. Place the bows evenly into six vases, staggered in height.

6. Insert the leather fern in every third vase or as needed for even color contrast.

7. Position the Floral Design at the desired location.

8. Add the glass disc to the center of the Floral Design.

9. Place three kerosene candles of different heights in the center of the arrangement. Light the candles for a dramatic and romantic effect!

Silk:

Without a doubt, this tree arrangement is really fun to create. The tree is made of silk pine sprays available in most craft shops or variety stores. The ornaments are regular Christmas tree ornaments and holiday picks, also from the craft shop. Just mix and match your favorite colors or themes to create your own personal touch. For this tree we used glass ornaments, candy canes, red bows and twinkle lights. We even used multicolored, mini Christmas tree lights. After lighting the tree, we topped it off with a light sprinkling of plastic snow.

1. Fill the Floral Seven and Floral Design with silica sand.
2. Fill each vase with two to three pine sprays or enough to make a bushy looking tree.
3. Position the tree at the desired location before decorating.
4. Drape a small cloth or use newspaper around the base to ease the clean up if you choose to sprinkle the tree with snow.
5. Decorate the tree as you would a regular Christmas tree, using a variety of small scale ornaments.
6. Gently drape a short section of twinkle lights around the tree. (Make sure you have positioned the tree near an electrical outlet if you plan to light the arrangement.)
7. For the final touch, sprinkle the tree/arrangement, lightly with artificial snow.
8. Remove the newspaper or cloth.

Dried:

The look of an old-fashioned country Christmas is created with a combination of red silk poinsettias, freeze dried leather fern, and dried baby's breath. Our focal point is a charming snowman candle, and the entire arrangement is contrasted with a red gingham place mat.

1. Using a funnel, fill the Floral Design with grits, .
2. Place one silk poinsettia in every third vase.
3. Add the leather leaf fern to every vase.
4. Use the baby's breath to fill the spaces between the poinsettias.
5. Add the glass disc to the center of the Floral Design.
6. Slip the red gingham placemat under the Floral Design.
7. Position the vase at the desired location.
8. Place the snowman candle in the center of the glass disc.

Food:

This lavish centerpiece is certain to have your guests complimenting you on your genius! They will never know how easy and quick it really is. Fresh pineapple, strawberries, red and green grapes and parsley are the ingredients for this masterpiece. The only equipment you will need are a few toothpicks.

1. Fill the Floral Design with fresh water.
2. Cut the parsley to four inch lengths.
3. Fill each vase with two or three sprigs of parsley.
4. Place a toothpick in the stem of twelve strawberries.
5. Place one strawberry pick in every top vase.
6. Position the Floral Design at the desired location.
7. Place a large pineapple in the center of the Floral Design. (Do not use glass disc)
8. Secure a toothpick in the pineapple at the base of the crown.
9. Drape a cluster of green grapes around the toothpick.
10. Repeat step nine, alternating red and green grape clusters until the entire pineapple is covered with grapes.
11. To hide the toothpicks in the pineapple, simply spear a strawberry, stem side down on to the toothpick and voila!

Happy Holidays!

BUDGET BOUQUETS

We feel there is no excuse for not having a beautiful floral centerpiece in the house at all times. It doesn't have to be a special occasion, especially if they can be made with little time and money!

Fresh:
The look of a fifty dollar arrangement can be achieved for pennies with this creation of fresh yellow daisies and trailing ivy.

1. Cut the daisy stems at eight inches. Remove all lower leaves but leave at least one or two leaves near the flower.
2. Fill all the vases with fresh water. Use both the Floral Design and Floral Seven.
3. Place ivy cuttings in each vase.
4. Place the glass disc in the center of the Floral Design and add the Floral Seven.
5. Add one daisy stem to each vase and fill any gaps or open spaces with an additional daisy.

Silk:

This may look like a seventy five dollar arrangement, but it is actually created with inexpensive yellow day lilies, that have several flowers per stem, and are available at your local variety store.

1. Clip the silk flower stems at fifeteen inches.

2. Fill the Floral Design and Floral Seven with grits using a funnel to expedite the process.

3. Place one stem in each vase.

4. Position the Floral Design at your desired location.

5. Add the glass disc to the Floral Design.

6. Place the Floral Seven on the glass disc, platform.

Dried:

The nostalgic look of a Victorian nosegay is created with these dried elements, many of which can be gathered and dried from your own garden! Eucalyptus, lavender heather, and wild mini gyp.

1. Using a funnel, fill the Floral Design and Floral Seven with silica sand, salt or grits,

2. Place Floral Seven on Floral Design using glass disc as a platform.

3. Make individual mini bouquets from the eucalyptus and heather. Surround them with a few stems of mini gyp.

4. Fill each vase with one mini bouquet until both vase units are complete.

5. Add more mini-gyp if there appear to be "holes" in the arrangement.

Food:

Chips and salsa are presented with a south of the border flair when combined with fresh parsley and beautiful red carnations. This easy to assemble centerpiece will surely have your guests commenting on your creativity.

1. Cut fresh parsley stems at four inches and cut the carnations slightly longer, about four and one-half inches.

2. Fill the Floral Design vases with fresh water.

3. Fill each vase with two to three sprigs of parsley. (depending on the fullness of the parsley).

4. Place four carnations in the top tier of the vases, equally spaced.

5. Place four carnations in the lower tier of the vases in the alternate spaces from the top tier.

6. Place the glass disc in the center of the Floral Design and situate at the desired location.

7. Place a large glass bowl of chips on the glass disc. (We have used a special chip and dip bowl which has a smaller dip bowl attached to the large bowl)

8. Fill a small bowl with fresh salsa, garnish with parsley or cilantro and place in the center of the chips.

INDEX

INDEX